Reading Essentials®
Exploring Science

Leveled content-area science books in Earth/Space Science, Life Science, Math in Science, Physical Science, Science and Technology, and Science as Inquiry for emergent, early, and fluent readers

Modern-Day Explorer
Written by Holly Jack

Text © by Perfection Learning® Corporation 2006

This Americanization of *Modern-Day Explorer* originally published in English in 2003 is published by arrangement with Oxford University Press.

Printed in China.

For information, contact

Perfection Learning® Corporation

1000 North Second Avenue, P.O. Box 500
Logan, Iowa 51546-0500.
Phone: 1-800-831-4190
Fax: 1-800-543-2745

perfectionlearning.com
PB ISBN 0-7891-6703-4
RLB ISBN 0-7569-6294-3

1 2 3 4 5 6 PP 11 10 09 08 07 06

Acknowledgements:

The Publisher would like to thank the following for permission to reproduce photographs:
Cover photography by Getty Images - News Services
Getty Images - News Services: pp 4, 7, 19, 21;
Tranz International Image Library - Corbis: pp 9, 11–12, 14–17

PERFECTION LEARNING®

Modern-Day Explorer:

Steve Fossett

Holly Jack

Contents

Introduction

Steve Fossett is a famous American adventurer. He has made many record-breaking hot-air balloon flights. He flew all the way around the world on his own. It took him seven tries to do this.

Steve Fossett now holds the world record for his flight. It took him only 14 days to fly nonstop around the world in his hot-air balloon.

Many people have tried-and-failed to fly hot-air balloons around the world. Hot-air ballooning is dangerous and difficult. Lots of things can go wrong. Some people have had to stop because of bad weather. Some people had problems with their balloons and had to land.

Steve Fossett reached his goal because he was determined not to give up until he succeeded.

First Attempt – 1996

On January 8, 1996, Steve Fossett set off in his balloon, *Solo Challenger*, from Rapid City, South Dakota. If all went well, he would be alone for three weeks in a space not much bigger than a closet. He would sleep for about four hours a day in 45-minute naps. He would have to breathe using special oxygen cylinders the whole time because he would be up so high.

*Steve Fossett in the balloon
before the journey*

However, things did not go well. Only three days after takeoff, Steve Fossett had problems with his balloon. Some of his equipment stopped working. He was forced to crash-land the balloon in a hayfield in New Brunswick in eastern Canada.

Second Attempt – 1997

Steve Fossett rebuilt his balloon and renamed it *Solo Spirit*.

On January 13, 1997, he launched again. This time he left from St. Louis, Missouri. He traveled eastward across the Atlantic Ocean and northern Africa.

People gather around Steve Fossett's balloon before takeoff.

Steve Fossett ate ready-to-eat meals that he warmed up. He used a bucket or bottle to go to the bathroom.

He flew for more than six days. Then he began to run low on fuel. He had to land in a mustard field in northern India. His balloon got caught in some trees. People from the local village helped him untangle it.

Steve Fossett set new ballooning records for distance and time. On his second attempt, he traveled 10,360 miles in 146 hours 44 minutes.

Steve Fossett after his unplanned landing in northern India

Third Attempt – 1997

On December 31, 1997, Steve Fossett tried again. *Solo Spirit* was launched from St. Louis, Missouri.

He had flown for over five days before he had more problems. The wind died down and the burners in his balloon stopped working. He was traveling over Russia. He had to get permission to land. He made an emergency landing in a wheat field near Krasnodar in southern Russia.

Steve Fossett sets out on his third attempt to fly solo around the world.

Fourth Attempt – 1998

On August 7, 1998, Steve Fossett tried once again. He did not want to give up. *Solo Spirit 3* was launched from Mendoza, Argentina.

He flew for nine days before he flew into a terrible thunderstorm. Lightning struck the balloon. *Solo Spirit 3* crashed 5½ miles down into the Coral Sea off the coast of Australia.

Helpers inside the balloon getting it ready for another solo-flight attempt

Steve Fossett is about to be lifted from the water.

Steve Fossett tracking the course of his fourth attempt

Steve Fossett was lucky to survive. He was knocked unconscious when the balloon hit the water. Luckily, he came to and dived out of the balloon capsule with a life raft. He floated in the life raft for 23 hours until the Australian navy picked him up.

He did not fly all the way around the world this time, but Steve Fossett did set another record. This time it was for the longest solo flight. On his fourth attempt, he had traveled 14,234 miles in 205 hours 59 minutes. He had beaten his previous record.

Per Lindstrand, Richard Branson, and Steve Fossett at the Marrakech airbase

Fifth Attempt – 1998

For his next attempt Steve Fossett joined Richard Branson and Per Lindstrand to fly in the balloon *ICO Global Challenge*.

On December 18,1998, the balloon was launched from Marrakech in Morocco. The three balloonists hoped it would fly them all the way around the world.

It did not happen. Six days later, bad winds forced the balloon to land in the Pacific Ocean, 10 miles off the Hawaiian island of Oahu. They had not achieved their goal.

Luckily, the U.S. Coast Guard picked them up after only ten minutes in the water.

In March 1999, two other balloonists became the first to travel nonstop around the world. Swiss pilot Bertrand Piccard and Englishman Brian Jones achieved this feat in 457 hours 49 minutes.

Steve Fossett preparing to launch his balloon

Sixth Attempt – 1998

On August 4, Steve Fossett tried for the sixth time to fly around the world, on his own again. He was more determined than ever. *Solo Spirit 3* launched from Northam in Western Australia.

Twelve days later, bad weather forced the balloon to land on a cattle ranch in Bagé, Brazil. It was just hours after Steve Fossett had crossed the halfway point. He had scrapes and bruises but was otherwise unhurt.

Steve Fossett after safe arrival in the Australian outback

Seventh Attempt – 2002

On June 18, 2002, *Spirit of Freedom* was launched from Northam in Western Australia. On July 3, Steve Fossett landed the balloon in the outback, southwest of Queensland, Australia. Finally, he had journeyed around the world successfully.

The giant silver *Spirit of Freedom* balloon was in tatters after the rough landing, but Steve Fossett was unhurt.

Steve Fossett had finally achieved his goal. After six attempts, he became the first person to fly solo around the world in a hot-air balloon.

This record-breaking flight took him 324 hours, 16 minutes, 13 seconds. The flight covered 20,520 miles.

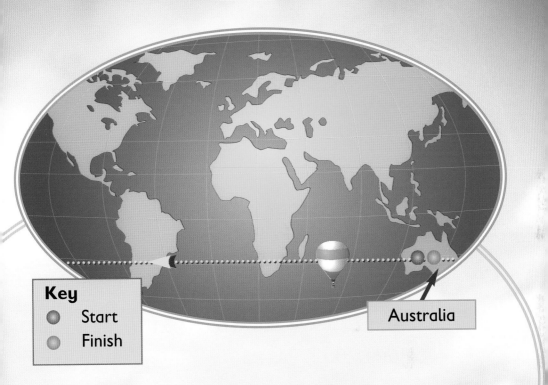

Key
- Start
- Finish

Australia

Now that Steve Fossett has achieved his goal, he does not intend to make any more long hot-air balloon flights. He is now planning his next adventure. What do you think it might be?

Index